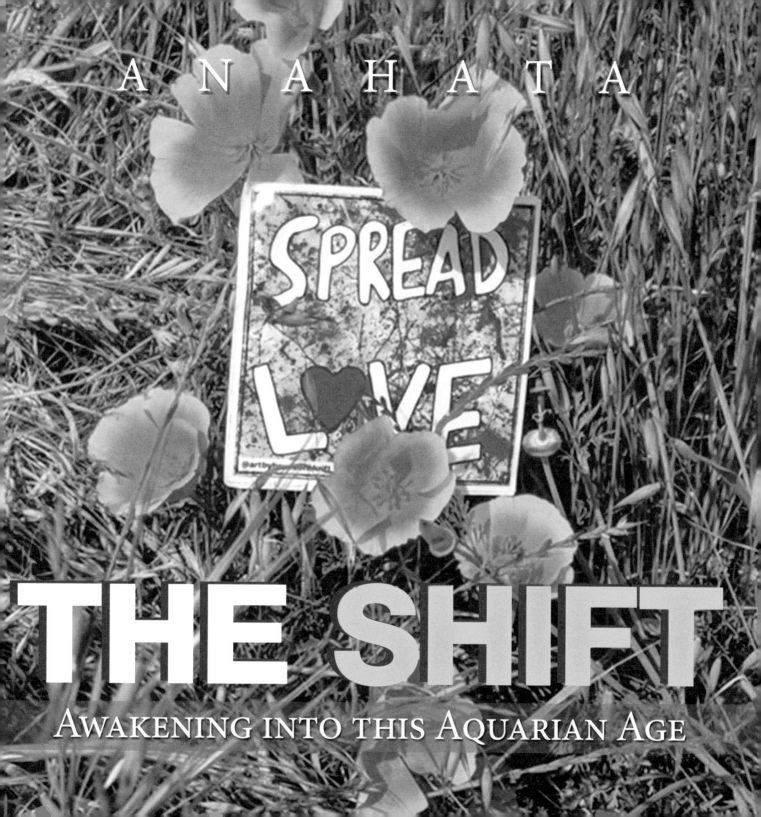

Balboa Press books may be ordered through booksellers or by contacting:

Balboa Press
A Division of Hay House
1663 Liberty Drive
Bloomington, IN 47403
www.balboapress.com
844-682-1282

Because of the dynamic nature of the Internet, any web addresses or links contained in this book may have changed since publication and may no longer be valid. The views expressed in this work are solely those of the author and do not necessarily reflect the views of the publisher, and the publisher hereby disclaims any responsibility for them.

Any people depicted in stock imagery provided by Getty Images are models, and such images are being used for illustrative purposes only.
Certain stock imagery © Getty Images.

ISBN: 978-1-9822-6866-4 (sc)
ISBN: 978-1-9822-6867-1 (e)

Print information available on the last page.

Balboa Press rev. date: 05/11/2021

BALBOA.PRESS
A DIVISION OF HAY HOUSE

Contents

FOREWORD

Her whole life, Julie has worked on spreading Love and Happiness, never once sharing anything that didn't promote such. She not only lives the life of Love, but it beams out of her when she's talking to you. She dedicates herself towards projecting out in the "Now Moment", "Love" in its most basic expression, and, in that magic moment it is created right then and there.

When you walk the path with her after meeting her, you can feel the energy she is putting out. It is such a breath of fresh air that no matter where you are, it brings you there in that moment with her. Then, you turn around and realize what a privilege it was to be in her company. Julie takes her time and looks you in the eye and listens to what you are saying. She then contemplates whether or not to give a comment. It's in that moment that there is a "Holy Instant" where you know that you met someone special on your path, who walks this earth, really caring about the people who walk with her.

Julie has taken paths where it was difficult for her to get from day to day but she never let you know just how difficult it was for her to do that. I would say she has great character and perseverance, while being very honest. She receives the better energy that life presents to all of us and then she shows you how to experience it for yourself.

Lou Marchetti, Author

THE SHIFT

Awakening Into This Aquarian Age

CHAPTER 1

INTRODUCTION TO THE AQUARIAN AGE

There is no substitution for the real thing and this time on Planet Earth is all about the real thing... Truth! As the Universal Law of Cause and Effect is fast at work, change is inevitable. When the earth shifts and changes, so too do her inhabitants - everything on Planet Earth. As one being heals, we all heal. In process of adapting, we become more heart centered beings and this brings forward a ripple effect that has an impact on those around us, and so on.

Throughout the times of the Ages there has always been one predominant trait or factor which describes that particular Age. The Piscean Age, which preceded this Aquarian Age was noted to be the Age of Automation. We are now ascending into the Aquarian Age, an age noted by the ancients as being an Era of Love. This is an era where in 'Love heals everything and Everything is Love.'

This love is like no other love and it resides within each and every human being on Planet Earth. As we are all here to graduate this 'Earth School' experience with the accomplishment of Self Mastery, Self Love is the prevailing goal of accomplishment.

Historically, putting one's love, care and attention on others has been the predominant characteristic of the times. If you know how nature functions, survival is the driving characteristic that brings mothers to care for themselves prior to caring for their young. The animal kingdom illustrates to us that in order to propagate the species, they must first take care of their own needs for survival.

As the Piscean Age evolved throughout the years prior to the year 2000, automation and industrialization became more predominant. Life was being drawn outward and away from just surviving. Over time, lifestyles began to shift and had evolved into multifaceted, thriving experiences where survival skills became obsolete. This, in turn, took the human experience outside of caring and nurturing one's self for survival to a lifestyle where life and living were being taken for granted. Focus was on thinking and doing things that had nothing to do with survival, death and dying, but had everything to do with living.

CHAPTER 2

AN OVERVIEW OF THE CHAKRAS

There are 7 primary chakras in the human body. These constitute what is known as the Sushumna energy channel. This energy channel runs up and down the front of the spine. Here, there is an energetic matrix where all energies of the body travel. As energy travels through this channel via the chakras, the body's 'dosha', or constitution, is derived. Dosha is a Sanskrit word meaning energy. Our dosha is dependent upon the energies that are predominant in each chakra.

Through these energy centers, traits of our entire physical being are homed. From food preferences to strengths and weaknesses, our chakras are the blue print of our physical world. The first of these 7 main chakras running up and down the front of the spine is the Root Chakra. This chakra is located at the base of the spine and is closest to the Earth. It holds our values relating to survival. These survival values include our need for food, water, shelter and mating.

The Second Chakra is the Sacral Chakra. From the front of the spine, this area is just below the navel center. This is where we house our values on creativity, sexuality and finances. The ideas and viewpoints we have about these subjects are imprinted in our bodies when we are very young and have a profound effect on our lives.

Just above the navel center, at the Solar Plexus, lies the Third Chakra. This is the power house of the human body. The steam engine to what drives and motivates us throughout our lives. Known as a place where we hold our imprint on motivation and self esteem, the Solar Plexus is also a location that houses our current values on self worth, productivity and inner strength. This chakra is formed during adolescence and transforms many times throughout our lives.

The Heart Chakra is the Fourth Chakra. It is the heart center of all of humanity. It is also the spiritual center of every human being and is located at the sternum in the center of the chest. The Fourth Chakra displays our openness and our willingness to love and to be loved. It drives humanity forward and is responsible for reproducing the human species.

Moving up the spine from the heart, lies the Fifth Chakra or the Throat Chakra. Located right at the center of the throat, this chakra is all about communication and speaking our truth. Vocalizing the voice of our authentic self and speaking from the heart are at the root of this chakra.

The Sixth Chakra, or Third Eye, is located at the space between the brows. This chakra is responsible for clarity in thought and intuition. Symptoms of a blocked Third Eye are headaches, dizziness and forgetfulness. This chakra is the main connection to the intuitive aspect of the human condition. This chakra is responsible for inner knowingness and our ability to foresee the future. During the Aquarian Shift on Planet Earth, this chakra is being transformed in all of humanity.

At the top of the head, or Crown, lies the Seventh Chakra. This chakra connects the physical human being to the Divine, or Source. Source is that aspect of ourselves which resides beyond our human comprehension. Often referred to as Creator or God, Source is what serves as our 'true north'. It is a guidance system of infinite intelligence which governs all of humanity.

CHAPTER 3

THE SHIFT

Welcome to the Aquarian Age. An Age noted by ancients throughout history and time to be an Era of Love. Where Love heals everything and every Thing is love. This is the Age of Aquarius and this is a time for celebration. During these early years, Planet Earth is moving forward through many shifts and changes. Also at this time, humanity is shifting and transforming one layer at a time. Just like the layers of an onion, the Earth and her inhabitants are shifting layer by layer.

With much unrest in humanity, it's no wonder the Earth and the constructs she inhabits, are experiencing tremendous changes and reconstruction at this time. All change is preceded by chaos and this chaos brings about transformation. So indeed, it is a time to rejoice and step forward triumphantly into this Age of Aquarius with a heart wide open. Be assured, there is great transformation on the way!

There are certain precepts and guidelines which serve to shape this new Age of Aquarius. Believe it or not, these precepts are even mentioned in the Bible during a time where 'heaven is on earth'. There are several grounding factors to this Era of Love, but 5 of them are at the top of the list and are predominant during these early years.

The first of these precepts is the Law of Attraction. If you are not familiar with this Universal Law, this law is the governing principle of all of existence. Simply put, this law states that 'Like attracts Like'. Plain and simple.

The second of these guiding principles entering into the Aquarian Age is the Boomerang Effect. The Boomerang Effect relates to Karma. It states, 'what we put out into the universe, we get back'. This precept is critical as we move forward into this new age of instant manifestation. For a peaceful and loving experience, it serves to be mindful of our thoughts, words and actions at all times. And, staying grounded and centered in our hearts is paramount for success.

Precept number 3 is the guiding principle that no two things shall be unique, in and of themselves. This is known as the Law of One. This Universal Law teaches us that we are all connected and we *are* all One, regardless of appearance or thought. This is a founding principle, as Planet Earth is shifting from an ego driven era where division and separation have been driving forces for much of humanity to a time where Unity Consciousness is at the forefront of this new age.

The fourth principle shares with us that no matter what, we have unconditional Love from Creator or Source. Everyone, every living thing on Planet Earth, has access to the Angel Realm which offers love, support and protection every minute of every day. In order to tap into this unconditional gift of love and support, all we have to do is ask.

The fifth precept and guiding principle in this Era of Love reveals to us, there are no accidents, mistakes or coincidences. We are navigating forward into an era of living with deliberate and instant manifestation. There are several tools we can use to guide and support a deliberate lifestyle and these will be discussed at another time.

CHAPTER 4

EVERYTHING IS ENERGY...
THE LAW OF ATTRACTION

As the first guiding precept into the Aquarian Age, its vital that we know and understand the Universal Law of Attraction. The principles of this Universal Law have been made popular and applicable through the teachings of Abraham-Hicks. If you are not familiar with these teachings, I highly recommend researching their valuable information. This information is pertinent to a successful transition into this new age.

The Law of Attraction teaches us about how 'like attracts like'. This can encompass any aspect of your life. On a vibrational level, our thoughts attract more of whatever we are thinking. As such, when thoughts are centered around joy, happiness and abundance, we get a joy filled, happy and abundant life experiences. It's really that simple. When we do something we enjoy doing, it sends out points of attraction through our field into the Universe. These points of attraction act like magnets that are holding that same joyful high vibration. This highly charged magnetic energy attracts more of what we enjoy! If our time and energy is not spent on high vibrational feeling 'stuff', according to the Law of Attraction, we attract and receive the lower vibrational experiences. Experiment with the Law of Attraction in your own life. Notice what you are thinking when you receive good news or when you experience a pleasant surprise. In contrast, take notice of your thoughts, energy and disposition when you encounter disappointment or sadness. Using this Universal Law to your advantage takes practice, but it is a sure thing to maintaining a happy and joyous life!

A successful tool you can incorporate immediately in your life is the use of affirmations. Affirmations are words or phrases with a strong message about what you want. An example of an affirmation that will attract positive, loving energy into your life is, "I intend to have only loving thoughts today and everyday. I intend to have only love in my life, today and everyday."

CHAPTER 5

THE UNIVERSAL LAW OF KARMA

What is Karma? Karma is the exact demonstration of the "Boomerang Effect". There are many different explanations of what Karma is, but the Boomerang Effect illustrates Karma in action. Simply put, Karma puts into reality a law of physics that demonstrates whatever is put out into space, returns. In our culture today, we know this as, 'whatever we put out into the Universe, eventually comes back to us'. There are several different aspects to Karma itself, but as it relates to forward movement into this Aquarian Age, the Boomerang Effect says it all.

Through awareness of our thoughts, words and actions we can assist ourselves in moving forward into this new age. As multi - dimensional beings living multiple lifetimes, karmic lessons are coming forward to us - to be healed in this new Era of Love. If you've ever met someone for the first time and that person seems familiar, chances are you are in a karmic agreement with that person. This agreement was made with those in your 'Soul Pod'. When you chose to incarnate into this life experience, you did so under the agreement that those in your 'Soul Pod' would be there to guide and assist you forward toward learning the lessons you chose to learn in this life experience. Whether you are wanting to learn about relationships or you are wanting to learn how to navigate through a particular situation, your 'Soul Pod' is there eternally and agreed to be there for you. This original karmic agreement was made before you incarnated into this lifetime.

There are several other details that factor into each Karmic relationship but for the purpose of this book, the Boomerang Effect is adequate.

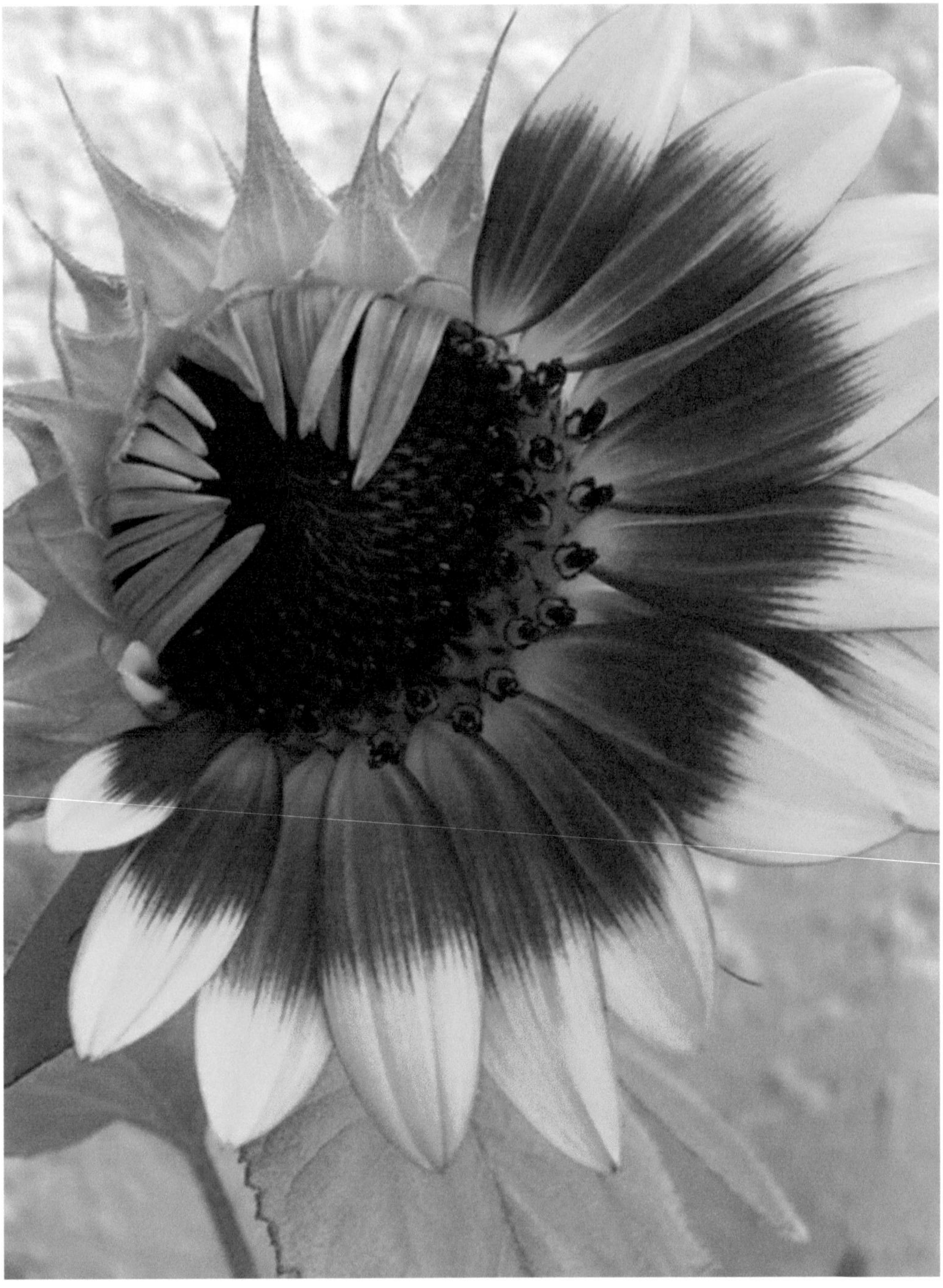

CHAPTER 6

OPENING TO YOUR HIGHER SELF

There are many different ways to refer to that greater aspect of ourselves. However you think of it or whatever you call it, now is the time to develop a relationship with the bigger part of you, your Source!

During this time of great change and transition on Planet Earth, having a connection to your spiritual self is valuable and integral for success. There are aspects of the human condition which are there for particular reasons. At this dynamic time of great change, these aspects of your being are poised and waiting for you to tune into them. They are commonly referred to as Source or God. For a successful integration into this Aquarian Age, what really matters is that you simply acknowledge that you are not alone. You have a whole team of Angels and Guides who are close to you, lovingly guiding you.

The concept of these Angels and Guides may seem far fetched to some, but if you are truthful with yourself, you have already communicated with them numerous times. Your 'team' consists of the Angel realm, deceased loved ones and Elementals. Elementals are from the Nature Kingdom and are here to support the earth's transition into this Aquarian Age. If you are reading this book, chances are, you are also here to support Planet Earth while transitioning into this Aquarian Age.

Many who are skeptical about these energies tend to not be able to successfully communicate with them. Prior to incarnating into this lifetime, you entered into an agreement with your team. This is a 'Sacred Contract' where your team agreed to guide and support you on your 'earth school' journey. If you open your mind to the idea that you are here with a host, a team of benevolent support, you are well equipped to move forward and thrive into this Aquarian Age... an era of Love.

So many before you have heard about this time as its been noted and talked about for centuries. However, it hasn't been until now, that we have reached a point where the change on Planet Earth is palpable.

CHAPTER 7

THE MOON - FEMININE ENERGY

The Divine Feminine has been getting a lot of talk lately. And, deservedly so. What is the Divine Feminine? The Divine Feminine is the Yin or feminine aspect of humanity. It resides within each and every human being. It encompasses the softer, more subtle qualities of the human condition.

The Divine Feminine energies support characteristics that are more nurturing and receptive. These energies are more in tune with the rhythm of life and going with the flow. The Divine Feminine teaches us that within all of life, lies a soul of love, peace and receptivity.

The relationship of the Divine Feminine to this Age of Aquarius is quite relevant in these early years. The cornerstone of this new age is marked by the Earth's axis taking a 2000 year journey, shifting from the sun toward the moon. This transition on Planet Earth is manifested through the tides turning from Yang to Yin. These changes can be observed in the changing characteristics of the weather and the behavioral changes of every living thing on our planet. The moon governs the weather and tides on Earth and the weather and tides govern the Earth's inhabitants.

Successful navigation through these changing patterns is dependent upon our ability to accept change and let go of what was.

ABOUT THE AUTHOR

Julie Klutinoty has been given the spiritual name of Anahata, Seed of Love.

Through her work as a Channel and Free Lance Writer, Anahata has been teaching and guiding humanity forward all her life. Starting with the more physical (body) modalities of healing such as yoga and Pilates, Anahata was guided into devoting her life's work to the progress of humanity. It was through her in depth practice of yoga and other physical healing tools, that Anahata came to know her true Self and her inner Being. Now, guided by the Angel Realm and Celestial Beings known as the 'Light Keepers', Anahata serves as a 'way shower' to those called to move forward into this Aquarian Age.

About the Artist

SPREAD LOVE cover art

I am Brandon Thrift.

Sarasota, Florida native, artist, musician and lover.

My 'Spread Love' journey began in early April 2020 amidst a global pandemic. From the ashes of mental tribulation, the necessity for cathartic rebelliousness and personal development, sprung forth an innate pursuit of youthful expressionism.

Utilizing my surroundings, I fueled my artistic fire with anything I could get my hands on - from broken down furniture, to used canvasses, mirrors and old bedsheets. In June, 2020 alone, I spent about a month on the road traveling over 13,000 miles from state to state sprinkling around hundreds 'Spread Love' pieces for people to receive the message.

Since then, I have continuously traveled to 43/50 United States sharing the fundamentally connective message of Love.

From the inception of this project, I have created and shared almost 3,000 individual pieces of art.